LIFE SKILLS

Well-Being

Written by
Steffi Cavell-Clarke

KidHaven
PUBLISHING

Published in 2027 by
KidHaven Publishing, an Imprint of Greenhaven Publishing, LLC
2544 Clinton St., Buffalo, NY 14224

Written by: Steffi Cavell-Clarke
Edited by: Beth Latham
Designed by: Rob Delph

Cataloging-in-Publication Data
Names: Cavell-Clarke, Steffi.
Title: Well-being / Steffi Cavell-Clarke.
Description: Buffalo, NY : KidHaven Publishing, 2027. | Series: Life skills | Includes glossary and index.
Identifiers: ISBN 9781534570580 (pbk.) | ISBN 9781534570597 (library bound) | ISBN 9781534570603 (ebook)
Subjects: LCSH: Well-being--Juvenile literature. | Self-care, Health--Juvenile literature. | Mind and body--Juvenile literature.
Classification: LCC RA777.C349 2027 | DDC 613--dc23

Printed in China

CPSIA compliance information: Batch #QS27KH: For further information contact Greenhaven Publishing LLC at 1-844-317-7404.

Please visit our website, www.greenhavenpublishing.com.
For a free color catalog of all our high-quality books,
call toll free 1-844-317-7404
or fax 1-844-317-7405.

Find us on

Image Credits

Images courtesy of Shutterstock.com, unless otherwise stated.
Cover and recurring – StockSmartStart, OLJ Studio, Alex Troi, WinWin artlab, A K O, ivector. 2–3 – Monkey Business Images. 4–5 – Zhuravlev Andrey, WESTOCK PRODUCTIONS, Volha Ye. 6–7 – GOLFX, Monkey Business Images. 8–9 – Roman Samborskyi, A K O, WinWin artlab, ivector, StockSmartStart. 10–11 – Shestakov Dmytro, BearFotos. 12–13 – BearFotos, Monkey Business Images. 14–15 – LightField Studios, Olga Kri, Colorfuel Studio. 16–17 – Yuganov Konstantin, Q88, Olga1818. 18–19 – takayuki, ViDI Studio. 20–21 – Asier Romero, Rido. 22–23 – ibragimova, KlingSup.

Contents

Words that look like <u>this</u> can be found in the glossary on page 24.

We Can Learn Life Skills!

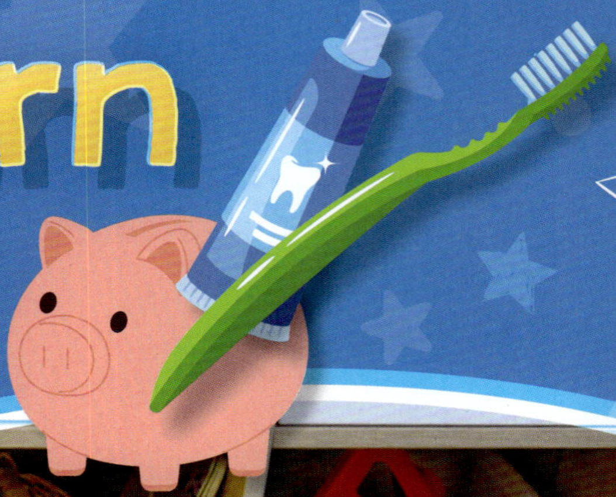

As you grow older, you learn life skills. These are ways of taking care of yourself and doing everyday tasks. Getting dressed, keeping clean, saying kind words, and neatness are all life skills.

Knowing how to look after yourself is an important life skill. Your body, mind, and feelings all need care to stay healthy and strong. Taking care of these things lets you enjoy the world around you.

EVERYONE DESERVES TO FEEL HAPPY AND SAFE.

What Is Well-Being?

Well-being is a state you reach when you care for your body and mind so you can feel your best. Creating healthy habits will help you care for yourself and help you grow into a happy and confident adult.

Taking care of your well-being means eating healthy food, sleeping well, moving your body, and having plenty of time to play and rest. It also means sharing your feelings and being kind to yourself and others.

A Healthy Body

A healthy body is a big part of your well-being. When your body feels strong and works well, it helps you feel happy and full of energy. When you have energy, you can do lots of fun things.

Eating balanced meals, moving your body, and keeping clean all help your body stay healthy.

Drinking water helps keep you focused.

Eating enough gives you energy to grow.

Keeping clean helps you feel your best.

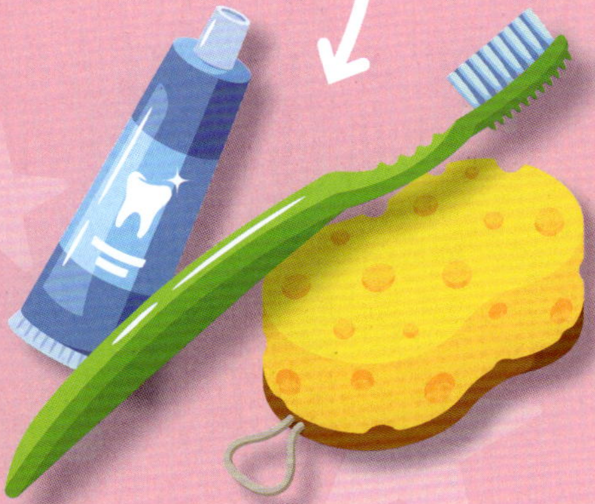

Movement helps keep you strong.

Moving Your Body

Moving your body helps your muscles and bones grow stronger. It also helps keep your heart healthy. There are lots of different ways to get moving, such as running, jumping, and swimming.

What is your favorite way to move?

Moving your body can make you feel good too. When you exercise, your brain releases chemicals that help you feel happy and calm. Movement can really help if you are feeling sad.

How do you feel after dancing to your favorite music?

Playing with Friends

HAVING FUN WITH FRIENDS IS ONE OF THE BEST WAYS TO FEEL GOOD.

Playing with friends is great for your well-being because it helps you feel happy and connected. When you play together, you learn to share, take turns, solve problems, and use your imagination.

Friends can help you feel supported when you are sad or worried. Spending time with others helps your brain grow in healthy ways. It also teaches kindness, teamwork, and respect.

Time to Rest

Everybody needs time to rest. Rest gives your body time to recover and your brain time to refresh. Our bodies need enough sleep to have energy to do all the things we want to do.

Getting a good night's sleep helps your body feel good. Resting during the day can help too. Listen to your body. If it is feeling tired, then it is time for a break.

Learning New Things

Learning new things is how you discover the world around you and gain new skills. Learning is important because it helps you make good choices and reach your goals in life.

Learning new things can make you feel confident and excited to discover more. It can be fun to solve problems, ask questions, and try something new.

READING HELPS YOU GROW YOUR IMAGINATION.

Sharing Your Feelings

It is OK to feel lots of emotions. Sometimes, you may feel happy. Other times, you might feel sad. Understanding your emotions can be tricky, but talking about how you feel can be very helpful.

Talk to someone you trust. They can listen, give advice, or just be there for you. When you talk about being sad, angry, or worried, it is easier for others to understand and help you.

Being Yourself

Being yourself means showing who you really are by sharing your thoughts and feelings. You should not try to be somebody else. Everyone is different. That makes the world interesting and fun.

Be confident in, proud of, and happy with who you are and all the things that you can achieve. You do not need to pretend. Just be yourself, because no one else in the whole world can be you!

Cooldown Time

Everybody has days where they do not feel their best. That is totally normal.

If you ever feel like this, here is a way to calm your thoughts and feelings. Breathe in through your nose and out through your mouth.

Take a few minutes to think about the world around you. Ask yourself these questions:

What can you see?

What can you touch?

What can you hear?

What can you smell?

What can you taste?

Glossary

ADVICE	an idea to help make a choice or decision
CHEMICALS	substances that can affect how something works
CONFIDENT	when someone believes in themselves or feels that they can do something well
CONNECTED	joined together
ENERGY	the power that makes living things able to move and live
FOCUSED	giving attention to a task or goal
HABITS	behaviors that people do regularly
RECOVER	feel better
RESPECT	feeling that something or someone is important
SUPPORTED	being helped by others

Index